CU00904397

MANAGING ACTIVITIES

CIPD REVISION GUIDE

Tina Stephens is the CIPD Chief Examiner for Managing Activities and Employee Reward. She is also a consultant in HR and Management Development.

Richard Pettinger is Lecturer in Management at University College, London, and has taught CIPD courses for many years. One of the pioneers of the CIPD's flexible learning scheme, he is the author of more than 30 books, many in the area of human resource management. Richard continues to act as primary consultant to organisations in the public, private and not-for-profit sectors.

The Chartered Institute of Personnel and Development is the leading publisher of books and reports for personnel and training professionals, students, and all those concerned with the effective management and development of people at work. For details of all our titles, please contact the publishing department:

tel: 020-8263 3387

fax: 020-8263 3850

e-mail: publish@cipd.co.uk

The catalogue of all CIPD titles can be viewed on all the CIPD website:

www.cipd.co.uk/bookstore

MANAGING ACTIVITIES

TINA STEPHENS

RICHARD PETTINGER

Chartered Institute of Personnel and Development

Published by the Chartered Institute of Personnel and Development,
CIPD House, Camp Road, London, SW19 4UX

First published 2003

Design by Pumpkin House, Cambridge

Typeset by Pumpkin House, Cambridge

Printed in Great Britain by The Cromwell Press, Trowbridge, Wiltshire

British Library Cataloguing in Publication Data
A catalogue of this publication is available from the British Library

ISBN 1 84398 020 7

The views expressed in this publication are the authors' own and may not necessarily reflect those of the CIPD.

The CIPD has made every effort to trace and acknowledge copyright holders. If any source has been overlooked, CIPD Enterprises would be pleased to redress this for future editions.

Chartered Institute of Personnel and Development,
CIPD House, Camp Road, London, SW19 4UX

Tel: 020 8971 9000   Fax: 020 8263 3333

Email: cipd@cipd.co.uk   Website: www.cipd.co.uk

Incorporated by Royal Charter   Registered Charity No. 1079797

CONTENTS

• LIST OF FIGURES

• INTRODUCTION

For several decades The Chartered Institute of Personnel and Development has been recognising professional status among those in People Management and Development through a programme of formal assessment. I (Tina Stephens) was examined under the IPM (as it was then) scheme that demanded success in a series of three-hour examinations covering such topics as statistics, economics, sociology and psychology, as well as training and development, personnel management and industrial relations.

Through two subsequent decades, the 1980s and 1990s, the requirements for assessment have not disappeared. The scheme has evolved with the profession in response to demands from HR specialists and practitioners, employers and candidates, from tutors and examiners and from the CIPD itself.

Major change has included:

- the introduction of the Professional Management Foundation Programme, now Core Management

- the requirement to complete an additional 'Stage III' Management report-style piece of applied research, which then became incorporated into the main scheme as the Management Report

- the introduction of new Standards in 1996, giving more emphasis to 'recognisable' people management and development areas such as employee relations, employee resourcing, employee development and employee reward and to associated Standards such as employment law, management development, pensions, performance management and selection and assessment centres.

The Professional Qualification Scheme, formally launched in the mid-1990s, set out the purpose and nature of the Standards:

■ PQS Professional Standards

'One of the key objectives of the Institute of Personnel and Development is the establishment, monitoring and promotion of standards and ethics for its profession. It has, therefore, defined standards across the whole spectrum of personnel and development, taking into account both generalist and specialist functions. In addition, these standards have been mapped against the National and Scottish Vocational Qualifications (N/SVQs), resulting in a structure which provides a wide variety of routes through which to qualify for IPD Membership'.[1]

The Professional Standards for Managing Activities were expressed through the following rationale statements:

■ Managing Activities

Rationale

'Managerial work is complex and fragmented in its nature. The very term implies a range of behaviour from administration to inspirational leadership, and job descriptions for managers may differ in the extreme. This module examines the various ways in which activities are managed within the workplace, including techniques, relationships and demands. The ability of the manager to communicate effectively is, of course, crucial and will be demonstrated through the learning outcomes, which require a variety of approaches.

'All of this takes place within a cultural and structural framework of the organisation in the current context of change for continuous improvement. As competition increases and resources become scarce, there is significant benefit to be gained from the understanding of how activities can and should be managed, including techniques, relationships and demands. This module is designed to enable such understanding and to facilitate the development of skills under three broad headings:

- The nature of managerial work

- The workplace environment

- Customers, quality and continuous improvement.' [2]

This redesigned Standard took account of the revised national Management Standards and saw two particular new areas: customers and quality and continuous improvement.

These national Management Standards are currently being reviewed, but it is not yet clear whether any major changes will be made. It would be expected that the CIPD Core Management Standards will also subsequently be reviewed.

There are a vast number of publications on all aspects of managing activities. Many of these are referred to later in this CIPD Revision Guide, but the student preparing for examination may not have time available to read so extensively. To help to narrow the options, the IPD published *Managing Activities* by Michael Armstrong in 1999[3]. This text follows the topic headings to be found in the Standard, and indexes these for ease of reference.

The Foreword to Armstrong's book, by the late Professor Ian Beardwell, notes that this is one of a series of texts designed to complement the Core Management syllabus.

'The role of the personnel and development practitioner has become an important part of the total management of all types of organisation in the private, public and voluntary sectors. A fundamental element of that role is the ability to comprehend and contribute to the overall goals, performance and outcomes of organisations. This is the purpose of the Core Management syllabus: to equip personnel and development practitioners to understand and appreciate complex business and managerial issues and to develop their skills so they can play a full role in that process.'[4]

Over the past two to three years, the CIPD has been reviewing its Standards and examination scheme. This process of review is ongoing, as good practice would demand. Thus far, the generalist and specialist electives have been reviewed, with Core Management on the agenda for Autumn 2003/Spring 2004.

This most recent review has led to some changes in the content of the Standards and to particularly noticeable changes in expectation for those taking the CIPD examinations from May 2003. The new Standard, commonly referred to as PDS (Professional Development Scheme), has a different 'feel' from its predecessor PQS. More emphasis is placed on continuing development, for example, in line with the CIPD's own values and those of its members. Chartered status is now awarded to successful candidates, still attainable through a variety of routes. Individual Chartered status will be available from autumn 2003.

Readers of this CIPD Revision Guide are likely to have embarked upon the journey towards becoming a Chartered member of their chosen profession. This will be no insignificant achievement. Those who have made this journey before will, no doubt, warn others that it is not easy, but will also have assured them that it is attainable and encouraged others to commence or continue. The revised CIPD Professional Standard has the following explanation in its introduction:

■ 'Revised CIPD Professional Standards

'One of the key objectives of the Chartered Institute of Personnel and Development is the establishment, monitoring and promotion of standards and ethics for the profession. The Institute has, therefore, defined Standards across the whole spectrum of personnel and development, taking into account both generalist and specialist functions. These Standards set out to define what a professional working in people management and development should be able to do, or should be able to understand and explain, if he or she is to operate at a professional level, at a support level, or at the level of an advanced practitioner[5].

'Effective performance

'Expectations about effective performance at work have changed radically over the past decade or so, and will continue to do so. It is now common (but by no means universal) for people to be recruited, selected, trained, developed, reviewed and rewarded against the degree to which they add value to the organisation that employs them. They can fulfil this added value in a number of ways, depending on the nature of the organisation, by:

- making a contribution, directly or indirectly, to organisational profitability

- facilitating the organisation's success in circumstances of corporate crisis

- helping the organisation to make progress towards vision and its strategic goals

- working in alignment with the organisation's mission

- customer-focused continuous improvement

- personal flexibility both when reacting to change and stimulating it.

'It is also much less common for people at work to entertain personal, automatic expectations about lifelong employment: they may be engaged on contractual terms which reflect the potentially transient nature of their relationship with the employer; they may, indeed, be working for organisations that are themselves deliberately transient, and they may be very well aware of the fact that if their employer's future is in jeopardy, then their employment is automatically at risk. Even if individuals are recruited by organisations that appear to have long-term futures, the possibility of significant disruption cannot be ignored. Many previously successful companies no longer exist, either at all, or in their original form; new types of enterprise continually emerge, especially in an environment dominated by e-commerce, globalisation and technological uncertainty operating in different ways, under new pressures and performance constraint.

'The CIPD publication, *People Make the Difference* (1995) argues that "personnel management professionals must add value to the organisations by which they are employed. To be efficient, they should ensure that all personnel systems, procedures and processes are characterised by efficient administration, compliance with the law, fairness and good practice. However, to be effective and genuinely add value, personnel professionals must:

- offer a high level of expertise in their professional field

- understand and critique the objectives and methodologies of their business colleagues

- import good practice from outside the organisation

- build strategic capabilities to optimise people performance

- develop and articulate the values of the organisation.

'The CIPD wishes to represent a profession that is taken seriously in the boardroom, which genuinely influences corporate strategy, and which contributes to bottom-line outcomes.'[6]

This CIPD Revision Guide includes important analysis of actual and suggested answers to real examination questions. It deals with content and approach, and will give candidates the confidence that makes them positive and successful. Managing Activities is important to all of us, it touches all our lives and dictates, for most of us, the quality of life both in and out of work.

REFERENCES

[1]Professional Standards, IPD, July 1999, p21

[2]Ibid

[3]ARMSTRONG M. Managing Activities, 1999, London, IPD

[4]Ibid

[5]Advanced Practitioner: one who uses the standards to build on the knowledge and competence gained at the practitioner level, probably as a Graduate or full member of the CIPD

[6]CIPD Professional Standards – Workbook for education providers of the Professional Development Scheme, 2002, London, CIPD

• GENERAL EXAMINATION GUIDANCE

This chapter offers guidance into successfully tackling the study of Managing Activities in preparation for the examination. It picks up on key features from the Introduction and the Standard itself, together with general, more generic advice about examination success.

Over the past three years, the CIPD has been revising its Standards. This has led to the introduction of the Professional Development Scheme on which readers of this CIPD Revision Guide are, or are about to be, enrolled. Before tackling an examination in any of the subject areas, there are some main principles to be internalised. These attitudes and approaches will be looked for by the examiner, in addition to knowledge of good and emergent practice. These principles come from the Professional Standards themselves and are the key to understanding the breadth and depth of knowledge required.

■ Key principles

These key principles are:

1   *Range of ability, knowledge, understanding:* what should a professional, working in people management and development, be able to do, understand and explain, if he or she is to operate at a professional level, at a support level, or at the level of an advanced practitioner?

2   *Added value:* either for the professional himself or herself, or in using management techniques and relationships to recognise and foster added value:

   • Making a contribution, directly or indirectly, to organisational profitability

   • Facilitating the organisation's success in circumstances of corporate crisis

   • Helping the organisation to make progress towards its vision and strategic goals

   • Working in alignment with the organisation's mission

- Being customer-focused – continuous improvement

- Having personal flexibility, both when reacting to change and stimulating it.

3 *Application of knowledge and skills across a variety of organisations:* while most candidates for examination are familiar with their own organisation and its policies and practices, those seeking success with the CIPD need to understand how different organisations work differently, and why.

4 *Relationship with the organisation:* candidates need to be able to respond not only to the size and nature of the organisation, but also in a variety of roles. They may be called upon to respond at board level or planning induction for new starters. They may be advising line managers on how to delegate effectively or negotiating with Health and Safety representatives over the potential conflict between production targets and safe ways of working.

5 *Working with change and uncertainty:* organisations today are in a constant state of change and transformation. A professional manager must be able to understand and advise through all the changes, start-up to closure, including changes in structure, culture and patterns of work.

6 *Maintaining standards:* ensuring that all managerial systems, procedures and processes are characterised by efficient administration, compliance with the law, fairness and good practice.

The IPD publication, *People Make the Difference* (1995), advises that the following capabilities are necessary for effectiveness:

- Offer a high level of expertise in their professional field

- Understand and critique the objectives and methodologies of their business colleagues

- Import good practice from outside the organisation

- Build strategic capabilities to optimise people performance

- Develop and articulate the values of the organisation.

7 *Ensuring 'best fit':* finally, it is essential that the management philosophy, policy, processes and procedures complement and support the other areas in the organisation, for example, a team culture is more readily achieved with team-based pay, team objectives and a group of employees who understand what teams are, how they work, and who perceive themselves to be a team. An organisation's structure and culture should be designed to enable success, whatever the sector or size. A bureaucracy is not the best environment for fostering creativity and innovation.

■ The CIPD's ten competencies

These values are also laid out in the CIPD's ten competencies for CIPD members:

1 Personal drive and effectiveness: the existence of a positive 'can-do' mentality, anxious to find ways round obstacles and willing to exploit all the available resources in order to accomplish objectives.

2 People management and leadership: the motivation of others (whether subordinates, colleagues, seniors or project team members) towards the achievement of shared goals not only through the application of formal authority, but also by personal role modelling, a collaborative approach, the establishment of professional credibility and the creation of reciprocal trust.

3 Business understanding: adoption of a corporate (not merely functional) perspective, including awareness of financial issues and accountabilities of business processes and operations, of 'customer' priorities (internal and external) and of the necessity for cost/benefit calculations when contemplating continuous improvement or transformational change.

4 Professional and ethical behaviour: possession of the professional skills and technical capabilities, specialist subject knowledge (especially legal) and the integrity in decision-making and operational activity that are required for effective achievement.

5 Added-value result achievement: a desire not only to concentrate solely on tasks, but rather to select meaningful accountabilities – to achieve goals that deliver added-value outcomes for the organisation, but simultaneously to comply with relevant legal and ethical obligations.

6 Continuing learning: commitment to continuing improvement and change by the application of self-managed learning techniques, supplemented where appropriate by deliberate, planned exposure to external learning sources (mentoring, coaching, etc).

7 Analytical and intuitive/creative thinking: application of a systematic approach to situational analysis, development of convincing business-focused action plans, and (where appropriate) the deployment of intuitive/creative thinking in order to generate innovative solutions and proactively seize opportunities.

8 'Customer' focus: concern for the perceptions of personnel and development customers, including (principally) the central directorate of the organisation; a willingness to solicit and act upon customer feedback as one of the foundations of performance improvement.

9   Strategic thinking: the capacity to create an achievable vision for the future, to foresee longer-term developments, to envisage options (and their probable consequences), to select sound courses of action, to rise above the day-to-day detail to challenge the status quo.

10 Communication, persuasion and interpersonal skills: the ability to transmit information to others, especially in written (report) form, both persuasively and cogently, display listening, comprehensive and understanding skills, plus sensitivity to the emotional, attitudinal and political aspects of corporate life.

In addition to knowing about Managing Activities, the successful candidate needs to demonstrate these competencies, if only as a backdrop to their answer. Later chapters take an in-depth look at the nature of the examination paper and its questions, showing how and where these values and competencies come into play. It is essential that the prospective candidate has these in mind during their course of study, not just at revision or exam time.

Before we leave the 'general context' area, there are two further approaches to be considered.

■ The Thinking Performer

The first of these approaches is the dimension of the 'Thinking Performer'. This phrase has been coined by Dr Ted Johns, himself a chief examiner for the CIPD.

The concept is visualised in the form of a grid. Our desirable 'thinking performer' is to be found in the top right-hand box and demonstrates:

- Personal drive and effectiveness

- People management and leadership

- Business understanding

- Professional and ethical competence

- Added value

- Continuing learning

- Analytical and intuitive and creative thinking

- Customer focus

- Strategic capabilities

- Good interpersonal skills

(The ten competencies highlighted by CIPD)

- **Figure 1:** The Thinking Performer

Thinking	The Wish List Dreamer or Fetish Fantasist	The Thinking Performer or Strategic Activist
	The Lifetime Liability	The Systems Bureaucrat or Corporate Policeman

Performing

This model is particularly helpful for those who would achieve success in examinations. Too many of our candidates answer questions from the perspective of Wish List, Lifetime Liability or Systems Bureaucrat.

The Wish List Dreamer – candidates here will often give a good account of theory and good practice, but ignore the practicalities of application. In their world, there are no difficult trade union negotiations, no opinionated chief executive officers, no demotivated process operators or clerical staff, no restriction on funds, no legislation, no business competition – in short, NO REALITY.

The Lifetime Liability is fortunately not someone likely to put themselves forward as a prospective CIPD examination candidate, but there are occasional glimpses of people working in the profession who are either so misinformed as to be dangerous or so unenthused that their answer to, say, the case study, amounts to no more than a paraphrasing of the situation as described on the question paper.

The Systems Bureaucrat is seen by many as the traditional perception of those in the People Management and Development profession. He or she is there to ensure rules and records are made and kept irrespective of the benefits to the organisation and its employees. The Systems Bureaucrat dimension is often encountered in examination scripts, and while this individual is, generally, not a liability as such, he or she is very limited in their outlook, questioning little, unaware of what is happening in other organisations, or of recent or emerging theory and research data. This approach is unlikely to meet the criteria for examination success.

Finally, it may be useful to prospective candidates to focus on the BACKUP analysis, which forms part of the examiner's criteria for judging scripts and will be used in conjunction with other guidance to communicate strengths and weakness to candidates who request examination feedback.

• **Figure 2:** BACKUP

Note: These assessments are derived from the five key **'BACKUP'** competencies which the examination is designed to test.

On the five-point scale used, 1 = Poor, 5 = Excellent and 3 = Acceptable.

COMPETENCY	EXPLANATION	1	2	3	4	5
Business Focus	An orientation towards results, continuous improvement and change – demonstration of the 'business partner' and 'thinking performer' perspectives, with people viewed primarily as added-value contributors to organisational performance.					
Application **C**apability	The willingness to address practical issues, exercise both analytical and creative capabilities, develop cost-effective solutions to problems, generate meaningful recommendations, design implementation and action programmes which convincingly translate higher purposes into tangible outcomes.					
Knowledge of the subject	A thorough grasp of the appropriate Indicative Content, familiarity with major theories, concepts, research evidence and new/current thinking about existing topics and emergent issues or themes.					
Understanding	Adoption of an appropriately critical and evaluative attitude to existing theory and practice, plus the ability to integrate research evidence into practical problem-solving scenarios and to make decisive judgments in circumstances characterised by ambiguity and incomplete information.					
Persuasion and presentation skills	The organisation of material, evidence, arguments, conclusions and action proposals in a manner which is systematic, lucid, cogent and businesslike, credibly constructed to fulfil the expectations of the visualised readership (both specialist and non-specialist).					

Again, the competencies reflect those expressed in the Introduction, the CIPD ten competencies and the description of the Thinking Performer. For candidates looking for a quick reference, this is a handy guide. When it comes to analysing ability to answer questions in a way that will gain good marks, a score of three to five in all categories should be the objective. All competencies are relevant to all parts of the paper, though, of course, some questions may focus on different aspects. For example, Business Focus and Application Capability will feature strongly in the case study, while one or more of the shorter 'Section B' questions may demand more emphasis on Knowledge and Persuasion.

■ The new PDS Standards

The new PDS Standards are more explicit in their reference and expectation in demonstrating 'M' or 'postgraduate' level. So, a major feature of the revised standards and accompanying assessment, by examination or otherwise, is the level of answers expected. This is best explained by descriptors, through which it is plain to see certain characteristics dominate. There is much debate in academic circles regarding what constitutes 'postgraduate', especially when it comes to professional or professionally related qualifications such as CIPD or MBA. The detail of this debate is unlikely to be of significance or interest to the prospective candidate. Suffice it to say the following descriptors are far more important. It is important to stress that these have always been sought in examination at PQS but are being more explicitly and openly required with PDS.

The CIPD Guidelines describe these thus:

'The criteria **all** postgraduates need to meet are:

- a systematic understanding of knowledge and critical awareness of current problems and/or new insights

- a comprehensive understanding of practice

- a conceptual understanding that enables the student to evaluate critically both current research and methodologies.

'This means that in responding to questions, candidates must demonstrate:

- a critical awareness of the role that contemporary personnel and development issues can play in the management of people and organisations

- a comprehensive understanding of how and why personnel and development initiatives may be appropriate in different organisational settings.

'They (the candidates) must show that they can:

- deal with complex issues both systematically and creatively

- make sound judgements in the absence of complete data

- be original in tackling and solving problems

- plan and advise on how to implement tasks at a professional equivalent level

- propose/make convincing decisions in complex and unpredictable situations

- communicate their conclusions clearly to non-specialist audiences.'

Figure 3 shows the generic descriptors for Distinction, Merit, Pass, Marginal Fail and Outright Fail.

- **Figure 3:** PDS Grade Profiles

Distinction	70% and above	(D)
Merit	60% – 69%	(M)
Pass	50% – 59%	(P)
Marginal Fail	45% – 49%	(MF) (Scripts confirmed as 45% to 49% by chief examiners will be referred to the CIPD to check against assignment mark and will normally then be considered for condonement at Moderation Committee)
Outright Fail	44% and below	(F)

Distinction   (70% and above)

* Comprehensive coverage of each aspect of the question – a completely focused answer
* Compelling evidence that the candidate thoroughly understands all the issues and can explain their full significance by reference to best practice
* In general, meets the highest professional standards in this area of the Standards.

Merit   (60% – 69%)

* Essential points have been covered and related as necessary to context
* Clear evidence that the candidate understands what the concepts/techniques referred to in the question mean, and their significance in broad terms
* A good explanation is given of each of the points made
* Overall, an answer that is not at distinction level, but that nonetheless is well balanced, impresses as being well informed and convincingly relates theory to practice where required.

Pass   (50% – 59%)

* Essential points have been covered
* Convinces as being useful and along the right lines even if some of the detail is sketchy
* Overall, an answer that deals with the main aspects of the question competently if not with any particular originality or flair.

Marginal Fail   (45% – 49%)

* The question has not been answered as set; and/or the answer is too generalised or thin and does not address enough of the specific issues raised by the question
* An answer that has potential, but on balance has some fundamental weaknesses that prevents it carrying enough conviction to justify a pass.

Outright Fail   (44% or less)

* An answer that is so flawed that it cannot be regarded as having even marginal potential. Does not demonstrate the level of competence expected in a qualified HR professional.

In making these requirements specific, examiners may have changed the phrasing of questions to make it clear to the candidate exactly what is required. For example, a Section B question might previously have read:

'Outline the major barriers to workplace communication in your organisation and say how they can be overcome.'

This question could now read:

'How do you get your staff to listen to you?' asks a colleague. 'With mine everything I say seems to go in one ear and out the other.' What constructive advice will you give her?

Examples of such questions, and suggested answers can be found in Chapter 4, but it is important to remember that if practising answering questions and using 'old-style' PQS question papers, the explicitness will not be so obvious. Reference to the list of competencies or to BACKUP will indicate what dimensions should be included in answers.

• THE CIPD's MANAGING ACTIVITIES GENERALIST STANDARD

■ Introduction

The purpose of this chapter is to provide an overview of the Managing Activities Generalist Standard and the broad field of management knowledge and practice to which it relates. The aim is to aid students' examination preparation by covering the seven performance indicators, indicating key areas, and providing references.

■ The CIPD's Managing Activities Standard

The Managing Activities Standard, like other CIPD Standards, breaks down into three parts:

Purpose

This gives the rationale for Managing Activities as a field of study and expertise, and explains the areas and ways of thinking and application required.

Performance Indicators

The Performance Indicators are both operational and knowledge based, so as to demonstrate the level and breadth of knowledge required, and also the ability to apply knowledge and expertise to a range of issues, at this level. It is additionally important to understand the particular context in which the expertise is to be applied, and that the nature of the applications varies between organisations as well as the present set of circumstances. The need, therefore, is to develop as full a range of understanding of each of the areas indicated below, and also to know and understand how each integrates with the others.

Indicative Content

The Indicative Content provides an outline of topics, skills, knowledge and expertise related to each of the Standard's seven Performance Indicators, and this is the basis of the coverage of this chapter. Additionally, these are the topics that appear in examinations, so they need to be well covered and clearly understood during courses of study.

It is very important to realise that this material is ultimately of value only if it has applications in practice. Do therefore study and revise from the point of view of understanding effective applications as well as theoretical knowledge. **The summaries at the end of each chapter of the core text are extremely valuable in this context.**

You must keep yourself up to date and aware of the full context in which management takes place. You should read *People Management* regularly. You should look at business and management journals. You should study the 'quality' press, news and current affairs programmes, and websites such as *www.ft.com* so as to keep yourself well informed and aware of current developments.

■ 1. The fragmented nature of managerial work

One of the main problems with all approaches to organisation and management is the need to try to make regular and predictable the fragmented, varied and disjointed range of tasks, pressures and priorities that actually exist and form the body of managerial and supervisory activity.

In practice this is rarely possible. Indeed, a key aspect of managerial capability and expertise is the ability to cope effectively with change and uncertainty. The need is therefore to instil and develop in all managers and supervisors the qualities and attitudes of flexibility, dynamism and responsiveness.

It is especially important to have positive and flexible attitudes to change, uncertainty, and problem and issue resolution. Managers may be required to switch from resolving customer relations issues, to staff problems, and then to production or service delivery quotas, in a very short space of time. The particular staff members, customers and other groups and colleagues involved expect their problems to be resolved whenever they arise.

See the core text, pages 5–18 for full details of the reasons and demands for this type of working.

Clearly, however, all organisations need their own structures and reporting relationships. Everyone needs to know where they stand in terms of their own rank, status, influence, authority, responsibility and accountability. Everyone also needs to know both the extent of what they can do, and the limitations within which they must operate.

Organisation charts and structures have great value as pictograms of the particular organisation, and its different departments, divisions and functions. It is, however, necessary also to see the limitations that charts have to offer, and the potential for divisions, conflicts and malfunctions that exist. When looking at organisation structures and charts, you should be considering the real and potential barriers to fully effective integration and activity. The specific barriers are:

- reporting relationships

- primary, secondary and hidden agendas

- political systems and alliances, and the reasons for the ways in which they work as they do

- formal and informal structures

- centralised and decentralised structures

- overtly conflicting priorities (eg sales need more staff to make targets; personnel/HR are required to keep staff costs down)

- competition for resources

- organisation culture and values, and management style

- locations, especially where some of these are close to sources of power and influence, and others are in remote locations

- matters of real and perceived status and influence with key figures in the hierarchy (especially senior managers).

See the core text, pages 131–132, 150–153 and 164–172. You should also make sure that you can give accurate definitions of specific terms, especially: culture; structure; centralisation; decentralisation; status; and influence.

The other key is the question of effective communication, and knowing and understanding all communication issues, especially the use of functional expertise, status and rank as barriers and distortions to effective and high-quality communications and information flows.

See the core text, pages 174–180.

Big issue: Flexible working

The key need is to see any flexible/non-standard working arrangements in the context of further fragmentation of the managerial environment, and also from the point of view of everyone involved:

- staff and the opportunities for enhanced ability to work, and to harmonise work with other life commitments

- customers and clients because of increased access to products and (especially) services at times convenient to them

- backers and investors, because of the ability to have technology and equipment in place and in use for longer periods of time

- overseas contacts, so that transactions can be made at times convenient to them

- the opportunity afforded by flexible and portable technology, enabling work to be done at any time and place at the convenience of all concerned.

Additional aspects to note include:

- the need for supervision of quality and volumes of work; the need for physical contact as well as e-mail and telephone

- the need for the effective use of all forms of communication with those on non-standard patterns of work and in remote locations

- the need for known, believed and perceived fairness to all – to those on flexible and non-standard patterns, as well as those working 'regular' hours and patterns

- the advantages and drawbacks of locating some activities in overseas and other remote locations (eg call centres in India; garment manufacture in Thailand and Cambodia)

- the advantages and disadvantages of specific approaches and different patterns, including: annualised hours; zero hours; flexitime; piecework/job and finish; and the demands made of people in flexible ways who remain on a standard salary.

See the core text, page 148. R Pettinger (2003) *Managing the Flexible Workforce* **(Thompson) is an additional useful source.**

2. Principal organisational functions and interactions

These are the standard and well-understood range, as follows:

- primary: production and services delivery (including professional services – eg teaching, nursing, medicine – in public services); operations management; research and development; marketing and sales functions; distribution; purchasing and the supply of components and raw materials and including access to databases; quality assurance and volume assurance

- support: HR and personnel; public relations; financial management; information systems and management; administration.

See the core text, pages 103–115.

These are supported by systems of communication, formal and informal meetings, cluster groups, consultation and negotiating forums.

You should note the circumstances in which organisations keep all of these functions under full control, and the present propensity for outsourcing particular activities, eg call centres, cleaning, catering and security.

You should understand the concept of core and peripheral organisations and workforces, and the opportunities and consequences present when choosing whether or not to outsource particular functions and activities. Note especially the problems of outsourcing in terms of loss of full control over both processes and outputs that occur as the result of putting things out to contract. It is additionally necessary to address the costs of resolving business and operational problems with contractors and specialists. Many organisations also find themselves from time to time addressing disputes between members of staff of the particular organisation and those of the contractor, and the costs that can be incurred when these disputes happen. **See the core text, pages 97-101.**

Big issue: Downsizing and Business Process Re-engineering

In recent years many organisations have gone through programmes of radical change. In a great many cases this has meant extensive job losses and restructuring, often carried out under the heading of Business Process Re-engineering (BPR). These approaches have been driven by: the need to remove expenses and overheads; demands from shareholders and backers that the payroll be no more than a particular percentage of capital employed; and by inefficiencies and blockages in systems, structures and reporting relationships.

This has in turn led organisations to concentrate attention on workforce size, structure and complexity, and the processes, systems and procedures both presently in place and operation, and also those required to make the organisation more effective. Many organisations have had extensive redundancy programmes. Elsewhere, staff have had to change their jobs, expertise, ways of working and reporting relationships.

It is essential to remember the behavioural effects of these and similar initiatives. These are:

- loss of full confidence in the continuity of employment and security; and these feelings persist among those who do not lose their jobs, because they wonder if it will be their turn next time

- loss of full confidence in senior management and those responsible for the organisation's direction and governance

- feelings of instability and uncertainty on the part of those who are to keep their jobs as well as those who leave in these circumstances. There is a primary need here for effective and good-quality information at all levels and activities. This is so that everyone knows where they stand as situations unfold, and so that as much productive work may be conducted under what are normally very difficult circumstances.

■ 3. Principal managerial tasks and interactions

The principal tasks are:

- leading and directing people, tasks, functions and activities, and setting clear standards and an example for others to follow

- achieving the desired, demanded and required results, setting and meeting targets and objectives, reporting progress (or lack of progress) and being able to explain clearly the reasons

- getting things done through people and having the necessary communication, decision-making, work allocation and prioritisation skills and awareness to do this

- delivering 'profit' in whatever terms that is measured and intended – finance, reputation, confidence, repeat business, overall and individual effectiveness

- developing staff, systems, culture, values and attitudes

- directing and setting priorities and deadlines; planning, co-ordinating, scheduling, organising, controlling and reporting in order to meet those priorities and deadlines; accommodating variations, changes and alterations

- dealing with crises and emergencies.

See the core text, Chapter 2, pages 22–45, and also pages 101–103, for a fully comprehensive explanation and discussion of each of these areas and how they are integrated. R. Pettinger (2001) *Mastering Management Skills* (Palgrave) is also a useful source for these areas.

Teams and groups

A critical area of management expertise is the ability to function as part of a team. This involves:

- the ability to build a team, and to understand the processes required – forming, storming, norming, performing; and also unforming, reforming, rejuvenation and ending. Remember the need to attend to:

  - processes and results – all groups and teams need early successes and achievements

  - the needs of individuals as well as the team as a whole, so that it is in everyone's interests to work effectively

  - the need for different roles, functions and qualities (**eg the Belbin approach – see core text, pages 79–80)**

- – the causes of dysfunction and lack of team and group effectiveness

- – individual and group development

- – the nature of leadership and management style, which must be suitable to the needs of the members, the organisation as a whole, and the nature of work being carried out

- the ability to work effectively in a team, both as member and also when necessary as a leader. It is especially important to understand the circumstances in which particular members may be asked to lead – eg where they have done a lot of work in a particular area, or when they are known or believed to have the greatest range of knowledge on a given subject among those present. **See the core text, pages 77–85, for full details on the ability to work effectively in a group, both as member and also as leader**

- the ability to arrange, conduct and manage meetings effectively. This means being prepared to chair the meeting, take the lead when necessary or desirable, ensure that minutes and records are kept and action points noted, and that these are followed up. **See the core text, pages 87–94, for full details on the structure, content and conduct of effective meetings, and the qualities required of the chair.**

Big issue: Mergers and takeovers

Exam questions about mergers and takeovers occur regularly. You need to be aware that 87 per cent of mergers and takeovers either fail or fall short of full success. This is because there is normally insufficient attention to the following:

- the need for cultural fit, integrating staff, structures and systems from two or more organisations into one that is now supposed to be more streamlined, flexible and responsive

- the need to integrate information systems, management styles and structures, reporting relationships, standards of product and service delivery

- the need to integrate and harmonise staff terms and conditions of employment, salary scales, benefits

- the need to generate a new and positive identity on the part of staff, customers, suppliers and shareholders, greater than, or at least equal to, that which they held for the previous separate organisations

- precise definitions in the particular set of circumstances of economies of scale, synergies, market entry, penetration and share; and the time needed to generate these targets, economies and efficiencies.

■ 4. Customer service

The primary need is to understand the basis on which internal and external customers do business with you. The keys are:

- identifying this basis, and identifying also their needs, wants, demands and expectations

- identifying the extent to which your customers are loyal, compliant or mercenary (ie they do business with you only because you are either the cheapest, most convenient, or best value)

- ensuring that either you at least meet each of their needs, wants, demands and expectations; or that you have other benefits which are at least the equivalent, or which transcend their demands.

For a full description of the basis for developing effective, enduring and profitable customer relationships, see the core text, pages 253–269. Another excellent source for this is R. Cartwright (2000) *Mastering Customer Relations* **(Palgrave).**

It is essential to develop and enhance customer relationships. The need is always to remember the reasons why customers come to you in preference to anyone else, and what customers want and expect from you. This applies to both internal and external customers. If you have preferred ways of delivering your products, services and functions, then these need to be tailored to the convenience of the people you are serving.

For example, if an internal customer needs information from you in a precise format, you can either deliver it in your preferred way, and then leave them to format it, or you can learn their format, and give a better service. If external customers require deliveries of materials, goods, products and services in their own ways, and you cannot or do not meet these ways, then they will do business with you only until someone else who can provide a better service comes along. This reinforces the need for all activities to be customer oriented, and service- and value-driven. **See the core text, page 124.**

It is critical to be able to anticipate, meet and exceed customer expectations. The only way to know and understand the needs, wants and expectations of customers is to go out and ask them. If you are asked this question in the exams, be as precise as you can about the questions that you would put to customers, and the reasons for asking them, and give examples wherever possible. **See the core text, pages 258–260.**

■ 5. Quality and continuous improvement

It is essential to understand the drives for continuous improvement and attention to quality. The specific areas to know, understand and be able to apply are:

- the meaning and importance of quality assurance: this varies between and within organisations. In general, it is essential to pay attention to all aspects of work – the materials, components and information bases used on the supply side; the processes used in the production of goods and delivery of services; the qualifications and expertise levels of the staff involved; the willingness, commitment and motivation of the staff as well as their capability

- the content, use and value of approaches such as Total Quality Management (TQM) and Benchmarking; the use and value of standards such as BS 5750, ISO 9000, and EFQM; and the use of terms such as 'kaizen'

- identifying the components of quality expected and anticipated by customers, and ensuring that these are delivered

- monitoring the quality of work: this means taking an active managerial responsibility to each of the aspects indicated above, so that everything is done in the best possible way in the circumstances, and so that problems are identified early and addressed immediately

- empowerment and support: if and when team and group members come up with suggestions for work improvement, these should always be evaluated. Some will be good ideas and workable; others good ideas and not workable; others bad ideas. The management priority here is to give effective and clear feedback, with reasons, on what is now to happen to the idea. This needs to be handled carefully and with respect. Bland responses such as 'the idea is now going through channels' invariably kill ideas, creativity, commitment and motivation. If the idea is not to be implemented for any reason, this should always be explained to the staff member or group face to face.

See the core text, pages 211–236, for full details. It is essential to realise that the quality of products, services and processes can always be enhanced and improved, and that this is what internal and external customers expect.

Note

From the points of view of both examinations and also practical reality, it is always essential to remember that if you are trying to convince senior managers of the need for particular quality or improvement initiatives to take place, they always need and want to know:

- how much it will cost, and what benefits and advantages are intended to accrue, and by when. You need to be able to give some figures and precise dates and deadlines in each case; and always avoid phrases such as: 'It is hoped' or 'We think' – senior managers dislike doing things on hopes or thoughts.

- what effects, if any, the proposal will have on present ranges of activities and patterns of work. If the answer is 'none', you need to make it clear why this is so; after all, most senior managers do not expect their staff to have a great deal of free time! If there are to be these effects, make them clear, and give indications how you expect to overcome them; and again, be as precise as you can, and avoid 'could' and 'might'.

- what you are recommending. Recommendations must always be prioritised, starting with the most important. Recommendations must always carry precise deadlines and timescales, so use phrases such as 'This is to be completed by 30 July' rather than 'This is to be completed as soon as possible' or 'This is to be completed as a matter of great urgency'. Recommendations must also carry resource implications; and again, be precise and use phrases such as 'This will cost £5 million' or, if necessary 'This will cost approximately £5 million', rather than 'There are likely to be significant sums involved'.

- if you are to make a full presentation. If you are asked to make a presentation to senior managers, you need to be able to convince them of your case in the first 10-15 minutes. If you are asked to do this as an exam question, you should structure the presentation for no longer than 30 minutes unless specifically asked to do so.

- what can possibly go wrong – and be explicit about this. If there are forecasts and projections, make reference to them. No certainty ever exists in any proposal. It is therefore essential to refer to probabilities and elements of risk.

You should make all of this clear if you are answering an exam question in this area. You need to be able to produce sample figures and timescales that bear some resemblance to reality. This in turn means having a good general knowledge of the sorts of figures and timescales that would apply (or have applied) in your organisation, others with which you are familiar, and examples that you have studied on courses.

■ 6. Change

All organisations are concerned with change, and all managers and supervisors have to be prepared, able and willing to work within this context. The key drivers are:

- financial: gaining increased returns on investment from present and finite levels of resources; making best and better use of cost bases, expertise, technology and equipment; targeting all initiatives with a financial objective as well as others concerning reputation, speed, effectiveness and quality enhancement

- culture, values and attitudes, usually concerned with generating feelings that are more positive, dynamic, inclusive and cohesive than those that presently exist. New attitudes and values must always be developed and reinforced when organisations are restructured, taken over or privatised; when there are extensive job losses; and when in-house functions are outsourced.

- behavioural: getting people to change and develop their work habits, output levels, ways of working and standards of behaviour and performance. The implications here are either that things are wrong and need to be put right; or that things that were right and effective in the past are now no longer appropriate and now need to be changed. If you are tackling an exam question on this subject, make it clear that you have thought of this. Make it clear also that the needs and drives for change must be communicated face to face, and supported by concise written statements produced with the full authority of the organisation

- competitive: the need to remain competitive in terms of maximising and optimising the cost and capital base on which activities are founded (and the budget base in public services); the need to develop new products and services; the need to produce effective innovations in processes and systems

- technological: the ability to assimilate and become effective on any new technology when it is introduced; to generate commitment to its usage from staff; to handle and manage glitches and problems when these arise; to ensure that staff are fully trained in its understanding and usage.

Remember the need to plan fully for change immediately it becomes apparent that these are to take place. You need to make it clear that proper aims, objectives and targets have to be set, and that full and open communications are required, so that everyone knows where they stand and what is expected of them.

See the core text, pages 274–284, for full details. See also pages 170–171 on the ability to deal with conflict when it arises as a part of the change process.

Big issue: The Internet and e-mail

The key attitude when considering the Internet is to ensure that it never becomes a substitute for enduring effective and hitherto profitable ways of doing business and conducting management practice. Both e-mail and the Internet are tools, to be used in support of the core activities of the organisation and its products and services.

The Internet has effective uses in advertising, the ability to generate a lot of contacts and information very quickly, and the ability to develop initial contacts and prospects to a degree not possible without incurring additional initial expense. The Internet is not, and will never be, a substitute for building effective and professional relationships with suppliers and customers and other key stakeholders and constituents.

E-mail is especially useful in putting out general information to all, and raising specific concerns. Full information can be put in front of people very quickly for any reason. Used effectively, e-mail should also speed up decision-making processes, through being able to set out clear and concise cases for executive action. However, if used wrongly, e-mail clouds and dilutes the quality of communications. Particular issues to be aware of include:

- information overload, in which people receive so much information that they take no notice of any of it

- lack of oral contact, in which the e-mail system becomes a substitute for telephone or face-to-face conversations that should be held

- avoiding key conversations such as those concerning radical changes, including job losses and redeployments.

This approach should be used in answering exam questions on this subject area, and also as a part of the answer to any question on the effectiveness and usage of all communication media.

■ 7. Health and Safety at Work

The key here is to remember the full complexity of Health and Safety at Work requirements and demands on all managers, as follows:

- approaches to prevention and cure: what to do when there are accidents and emergencies, and creating the conditions in which accidents and emergencies are kept to a minimum

- attitudes: creating and instilling the required attitudes and standards at the induction stage, and making sure that these are reinforced with behaviour and procedures applied across the board; and making sure always that proven and demonstrated breaches of health and safety procedures and practices are treated as disciplinary issues

- procedures: general procedures for emergencies and drills that apply to everyone regardless of rank, status, position or length of service; and specific procedures that govern everything that requires them, including: clothing (for extremes of danger, dirt, dust, heat and cold); use of VDU screens and time away from them; any and all equipment usage

- training in safe general practices (which also reinforces the desired and required attitudes); training in specific issues including: manual handling; lifting; environmental awareness; knowledge of emergency escape routes.

Note

From the points of view of both examinations and also workplace practice, whenever you are asked to produce the outline for a safety training course or briefing, always remember to include:

- specific aims and objectives

- the nature, rank, status and occupations of those who are to attend (and you should be realistic here – eg if you are asked to put on a session for senior managers, you will not in practice get them to stay for more than 1–2 hours unless there is an overwhelming strategic concern)

- length of the course (and be realistic here – you can do only so much in an hour/day/week, and you should prioritise and structure the material accordingly)

- mix of activities

- allowances for discussions.

General attention is additionally required in the areas of:

- legislation covering general health and safety at work; and specific laws and regulations – COSHH; manual handling; toxic substances; the role and function of the HSE – powers of inspection, duties and responsibilities; and the responses of the HSE to accidents and emergencies

- recording: the need to maintain complete and accurate records on all aspects of health and safety at work; the need to record and report serious accidents, injuries and illnesses; the need to record all absences on grounds of illness and injury, including self-certification, and to conduct returner interviews when individuals come back to work.

See the core text, pages 186–210, for a full coverage of these issues. The Health and Safety Executive website www.hse.org.uk is also a very useful source of information.

Big issue: Stress

Workplace stress is a major present concern for all organisations and their managers. The need for all organisations is to understand where the causes of stress lie in their particular situation, and what – if anything – they can do about it. Stress presently costs UK industry, commerce and public services a total of £16 billion per annum in lost production and output. The full range of actual and potential causes and sources of stress is very wide-ranging, and their mix and prevalence varies between and within organisations. The main areas include: bad working practices; bad and dishonest management and supervisory styles; bad employee and interdepartmental relations; alienation and remoteness of working relations and inclusion; long hours; insufficient resources; disharmony between management and other organisational drives (a serious problem in UK public services at present). If you are asked in an exam question (or at work) to produce an outline approach to tackle workplace stress, make sure that you cover each of these points, the actual and potential costs, and the likely and possible consequences for organisational and operational effectiveness.

■ Conclusion

The purpose of this chapter has been to cover the material of the Managing Activities Generalist Standard in a clear, concise and orderly way, giving clear points of reference to the core text and other sources. Each of the Standard's operational and knowledge indicators is covered. The additional material – the 'big issues' and the notes – is there to enhance your approach to current organisational and managerial concerns, and to give you a structure on which to base effective examination answers (and also to begin to deal with these issues when they arise at the workplace).

Chapter 3 now builds on this material further in the particular context of the Managing Activities examination.

• GUIDANCE TO CANDIDATES FROM CIPD EXAMINERS

It is important to approach preparing for study and examinations together because:

- it will enable selectivity in study and training the mind to assimilate knowledge in a form that will allow it to be easily retrieved

- although the longer-term aim is to become a competent professional, it is necessary to pass that examination and, as a major step forward, parameters and demands must be understood from the very beginning.

Whether the chosen method of study is through attendance at a college or university, or by distance learning, all candidates need to make themselves familiar with the standard and with the examination question paper. (Not the actual one to be taken, unfortunately!) In addition, there will be recommended reading lists that include a range of sources, from books to websites.

■ The Standard

The Managing Activities Standard is divided into sections:

Purpose

This explains the rationale and relevance of Managing Activities.

Performance Indicators

These are divided into two sections, Operational Indicators and Knowledge Indicators. It is recognised that candidates vary; some are more senior than others, some have less experience of different types of organisation, some have significant line management or supervisory experience.

The Operational Indicators (OI) for Managing Activities range over seven aspects of the manager's role. Practitioners must be able to:

- prepare an organisational chart and identify the way in which the organisation could be improved to make it work more efficiently and effectively

- work effectively in a group or team in a variety of roles

- prioritise, plan and delegate a variety of tasks

- prepare and deliver a convincing proposal/argument in a variety of situations

- contribute to the design and gain acceptance of a programme of change

- design and gain acceptance of a planned programme for improvement of service to internal/external customers

- advise a specified group of staff on the importance of health and safety in the workplace, outlining minimum organisational and legislative requirements

The Knowledge Indicators (KI) for Managing Activities require practitioners to know about and be able to explain:

- the fragmented nature of managerial work

- the principal functions in an organisation and how they interact

- the ways in which managers interact with and respond to others in the work organisation, particularly senior management, peers and subordinates

- the importance and method of achievement of good service to customers

- the requirements and implications of quality and continuous improvement

- the elements that lead to the successful introduction of change

- the need for a safe and healthy workplace environment.

On reviewing the operational indicators in the Standard it will be noticed that the words contribute, assist, participate and advise are frequently used. This demonstrates that candidates are not expected to be able to do all these things on their own, but still requires them to be a Thinking Performer rather than a Lifetime Liability! Knowledge indicators (KI) are just that, and outline the core of the information that needs to be known and remembered. The chosen study programme should have these included. When examination papers are set, they will cover *all* aspects of the operational and knowledge indicators, sometimes combining them just to make life more difficult.

For example, it would be possible that Operational Indicator (OI) 5, 'Contribute to the design and gain acceptance of a programme of change', might be combined with Knowledge Indicator (KI) 7, 'the need for a safe and healthy working environment', in a question that asks about introducing or reviving safe working practices. The answer to this question would also draw on KI 6, 'the elements that lead to the successful introduction of change'.

The third part of the Standard is Indicative Content (IC). This section is there to give a further guide to the knowledge requirements. It is a very comprehensive list, but can be updated only every so often, so there also is a need to keep up to date with more recent data through journals, quality newspapers, websites, conferences and seminars. Michael Armstrong's text *Managing Activities* is conveniently divided into parts that reflect the sections in the Indicative Content, which should aid the study plan.

■ The examination question paper

The sooner prospective candidates familiarise themselves with the general layout of the paper, the better. Get to know the style of questions and try to answer some of them. This can test learning and memory as time goes on, but at the start it can help to establish what is and is not known, thus leading into reading and other enquiry to 'get up to speed'.

Managing Activities is a two-section paper that allows ten minutes initial reading and two hours to answer the questions. It is crucial that time is well managed. Both sections carry equal marks so it is foolish to spend 90 minutes on one section and only 30 minutes on the other.

Section A

This section is designed to test both Operational and Knowledge Indicators. It addresses all the ten competencies from the CIPD and BACKUP checklists. Section A comprises three questions, of which the candidate must answer two. A review of previous (PQS) papers will reveal that the topics for the question may be taken from any part of the standard. With 30 minutes allowed for each Section A answer, there is opportunity for the examiner to place quite complex demands on the candidate. It is common in Section A questions for candidates to be given a specific role and or format for their response. For example, 'you are to lead a working party' or 'you are coaching a small group of management trainees' and 'prepare a checklist for supervisor' or 'outline a presentation for senior managers in our organisation which will convince them that ...'. A useful tip with Section A questions is that they tend to focus on change, changing attitudes and behaviours in particular. They will also, therefore, look for arguments to be persuasive and supported by evidence that the anticipated change will lead to successful outcomes. Such phrases as 'convince' and 'gain acceptance' are common. It is important to address the role, context and task in the answer, as marks will be allocated for all of them. An 'essay' on the theory of change or the benefits of safe working practices, no matter how thorough, will not gain as good a mark as it should if the question asks for that information set out as a checklist or in the form of a presentation.

Section B

This section contains ten questions, of which seven must be answered. Failure to answer seven will result in automatic failure on the paper as a whole.

These questions will be more situational, often requiring a rapid, brief response: the kind of question colleagues might phone or e-mail about, or ask in the corridor or car park. Other questions in Section B may fall between immediate response and miniature case study (in five or six lines). The questions still incorporate operational and knowledge indicators and will ask for a significant variety of types of response. It is essential to read through all ten questions in the examination. They often combine different areas of the standard where candidates may be confident in one area and not the other. Questions may ask for a form of response that candidates are not confident about, even though you know the topic thoroughly. It is not advisable to wade in where just a word or phrase is recognised.

A detailed analysis of the May 2003 paper can be found in Chapter 4, which gives further guidance on each question and indicative examples of good answers.

■ Reading and data sources

All reading and research needs to be focused, and guidance may be given by your tutor. Management is a broad topic. and candidates may be fazed by the potential number of texts available. This can be especially bewildering if there is infrequent library access, as may be the case with part-time students. There are some classics, such as Handy, *Understanding Organisations* (1985),[1] or Kanter, *The Change Masters* (1984)[2] that will always appear on any reading list. Even earlier texts such as Stewart, *Managers and their Jobs* (1967)[3] are worth dipping into. There are, however, a growing number of new and up-to-date publications, and the best advice is to go for the most recent sources of information. A recently published general management text is likely to include some review of the standard 'classic' writers to serve as a reminder of the basics. There are also texts whose purpose is to summarise, for example, Pugh and Hickson, *Writers on Organisations* (1996).[4]

General texts

Managing Activities by Michael Armstrong is one of a series of texts written specifically to complement the Core Management Standards. 'Michael Armstrong demonstrates that operating as an effective manager requires a clear appreciation of the nature of managerial work, its location in the structure, functions and power relationships within organisations, and an ability to comprehend and operate in the context of change, improvement and customer care.'[5] The author notes that the aim of the book has been 'to provide a general introduction into all aspects of managing a business and the activities carried out within a business. The book is structured around the core management professional standards, developed by the (then) Institute of Personnel and Development for "Managing Activities". These in turn, were influenced by the NVQ definitions for their managerial modules, especially those designed for Level 4. The book also takes account of the management standards produced by the Management Charter Initiative (MCI).' Other good general texts include: Armstrong M., *How to Become an Even Better Manager*. 5th edn, 1999, Kogan Page.

Although there are many texts with 'management' in the title, students might also want to seek out texts on customer care and service, on health and safety, and on quality and continuous improvement.

Textbooks are by definition somewhat out of date by the time they are published, so it is essential to keep up to date with journals and websites.

Journals

All student members of the CIPD will receive *People Management*, which regularly contains management-related items and updates, as do many of the general HR academic publications. IDS is an excellent source of up-to-date information, with critical views on new initiatives and updates on developments in practice.

Harvard Business Review is another well-respected journal in the field.

Websites

In addition to the CIPD website and those associated with IDS and HBR mentioned above, there are some consulting websites offering access to materials and case studies. DTI, DfEE and The Work Foundation (Industrial Society) also provide up-to-date recent developments and critiques.

CPD CD-Rom

If prospective students are not sure about the Professional Standards or how much they already know, the CIPD's CPD CD-ROM has a diagnostic questionnaire that can help. This will aid in planning study and reading requirements.

- Do not expect to read/learn everything at once!

- Plan the reading over the duration of study.

- Collect copies of journal and newspaper articles and file them until needed.

- After reading a chapter in the text, make brief notes of the main points, or answer a question from a past paper. This will help to consolidate the knowledge and enable you to check to see how much you have retained. It is too late to start to read everything all over again in the run-up to the examination.

■ Revision

Success in both study and at the examination is strongly influenced by the level of confidence in one's self and one's ability to pass. This confidence can be enhanced in two areas: confidence that one has the knowledge needed, and confidence that one can manage the process of revision and the examination itself.

Many students make a huge mistake from the beginning of their studies in that they fail to start learning early enough. This learning begins for many only during what they call revision.

It is hoped that the first reading of this CIPD Revision Guide is at the commencement of studies and not in the weeks and days immediately before the exam.

There will be much listening and note-taking throughout the course of study, together with private research and reading, but it is essential to start learning at the beginning. This is not a holiday novel scenario, where it does not really matter if at the end, or a few weeks later, the name of the heroine or the nationality of the villain is forgotten. In order to pass the examination, candidates have to remember what they have been taught, by themselves or others, and to be able to apply that knowledge to a new situation or different context. So it is not enough to know vaguely that knowledge must be thorough. The Standard covers a wide range of material, all topic-related, and when setting the examination question papers chief examiners are required to cover the whole range, so there will always be a question on some aspect or other of all of it. In their guide to examination success, *The examination experience and how to make it work for you*, which is included in every examiner's report, Ted Johns and Tina Stephens recommend:

- Know at least 50 per cent of the Standard Indicative Content in detail and the other 50 per cent more superficially (so that you can say something sensible about any topic at all).

- Know the current, and emergent, research, theory and writers in the area, not necessarily in detail, but sufficiently well as to be able to make reference to them. This underlines the 'thinking' dimension of the thinking performer.

- Know how personnel management and development is 'done' in a variety of scenarios, eg public/private/voluntary/manufacturing/service/local/ national/ international. This underlines the 'performing' dimension.

Everyone has their own preferred approach to revision, but without having gathered a body of knowledge there won't be much to revise! What to revise, how and where, are important choices to make. Structuring the material and scheduling the revision will help, whatever the preferred style. Give some thought too to the presentation of material. While there may be a vast array of books, notes and articles, these all need to be read, which is time-consuming. What about making audio tapes of the notes or main points that can be listened to in the car, or on the Walkman while sitting on the train or walking the dog? If mind maps are used for notes or revision, draw them up extra large on flip chart or A3 paper and stick them up around the house as a constant reminder while the household chores are done, or breakfast eaten. To pass these exams first time it is vital to make these preparations.

The other vital ingredient is to test out the learning. It is not worth leaving to chance and hoping that it can be recalled 'on the day', so 'KNOW YOU KNOW IT'. Students must self-test, or get someone else to test them, on the main points about each topic. Using questions from past papers is helpful, as it will also test knowledge and ability in a variety of contexts and topic combinations. It is important to include tests on the areas where more confidence is felt, as well as those that are very new. Just because the candidate's main employment is as a recruitment interviewer or union negotiator, it cannot be assumed that there is no need for extra learning or revision. This qualification we are dealing with here is forward looking, not so much what is currently done, more about what will be done in the future, maybe in a different organisation or at a higher level. Finally, notes must be organised in a way that breaks the material into smaller chunks to aid learning. It might be sensible to do this under the headings found in the Indicative Content of the Standard itself.

The nature of managerial work

- Fragmentation, variety, brevity and diversity; reasons for the prevalence of this kind of working.

- Prioritisation, allocation of work and delegation, the organisation of work.

- Working for other people, responding to objectives, meeting deadlines, report writing, written/oral presentation and influencing techniques.

- Working effectively in a group or team as a member or leader, the nature of meetings, working parties, committees. Chairing meetings, team-building.

- Communications: purposes, processes and barriers.

The work environment

- The principal function in an organisation, roles, objectives and key activities; research and development, marketing and sales, operational and production, purchasing, finance, personnel and development.

- Organisational culture, structure and design. Different forms of structure: formal, informal, centralised, decentralised, divisionalised, specialisation and autonomy, value-driven, customer focus, service orientation. Organisational conflict, politics, power and authority.

- Promotion and importance of health and safety in the workplace: procedures, records, organisational and legislative requirements.

- Assessment of working conditions, industrial and professional codes of practice relevant to healthy, safe and productive work environments; responding to contradictions between health and safety requirements and organisational constraints.

Quality and continuous improvement

- The meaning and importance of quality assurance, monitoring quality of work.

- Empowering team members to make recommendations on quality improvement and efficiency and how to encourage their contributions.

- Developing and enhancing internal and external customer relationships, anticipating and exceeding customer expectations.

- Achieving change; identifying options, handling conflict, overcoming resistance.

A further category should be added to pick up on very recent ideas:

- Hot topics.

Use the textbook

Another approach would be to structure all revision under the headings of the sections of Michael Armstrong's *Managing Activities*.[6] The book is divided into three parts with 16 subsections. They are:

- what managers do – fragmentation, variety, brevity

- the conduct of managerial work

- working for other people

- communicating with other people

- teamwork

- meetings

- the principal functions in an organisation

- organisational culture

- organisation structure, design and development

- power, authority, politics and conflict in organisations

- organisational communications

- managing health and safety at work

- managing and achieving quality

- continuous improvement

- customer care

- change management.

The utilisation of either of these sets of headings will ensure that the standard is covered. Candidates must know at least half of it thoroughly and the other half fairly well.

Finally, memorise in some diagrammatic form the Managing Activities standard as a whole.

The determination of the structure and headings will enable the organisation of materials and begin the filtering and learning process that will lead to a position where there are a manageable number of facts and illustrations for candidates to take into the examination room in their head. Most students use their revision to condense information down further and further, giving themselves brief notes to review immediately before their examination.

A revision schedule

When to begin this revision is again up to the individual, but an obvious general piece of advice is not to leave it all until the last minute. It is necessary to allow for such eventualities as unexpected visitors, bouts of hay fever, crises at work, sick children or partners and Bank Holidays. Fresh air and relaxation are also important, as for many students just 'getting started' is the hardest part. A timetable for the weeks leading up to the examination will not only help to stay on track, it will also give a psychological boost through the feeling of having made a start! Everything will need to be gone over at least three times in the filtering exercise, though the time that takes will decrease. First and last on the schedule should be the wider picture, with the detailed aspects in the middle part. So it might look like this if Armstrong's sections were to be followed:

Week	Topic
1)	What managers do (1)
	The conduct of managerial work (1)
	Working for other people (1)
	Communicating with other people (1)
2)	Teamwork (1)
	Meetings (1)
	Principal functions (1)
	Organisational culture (1)
3)	Organisation structure, design and development (1)
	Power, authority, politics and conflict (1)
	Organisational communications (1)
4)	Managing Health and Safety at Work (1)
	Managing and achieving quality (1)
	Continuous improvement (1)
	Customer care (1)
	Change management (1)
5)	What managers do, the conduct of managerial work (2)
	Working for and communicating with other people (2)
	Teamwork, meetings (2)
6)	Principal functions in an organisation (2)
	Organisation culture, structure, design and development (2)
	Power, authority, politics and conflict (2)
	Communication in organisations (2)
	Managing Health and Safety at Work (2)
7)	Managing and achieving quality (2)
	Continuous improvement (2)
	Customer care (2)
	Change management (2)
	What managers do, the conduct of managerial work (3).

By now, it may be sensible to concentrate on some topics more than others, so the list might reduce for the final filter in week eight to:

8)   Working and communicating with other people (3)

            Organisational culture, structure, design and development (3)

            Continuous improvement (3)

            Customer care (3)

            Change management (3).

The first round (1) ensures that all relevant materials are together, lecture notes, articles, typical questions and so on. Going through these, it can help to make key words and phrases with a highlighter pen or, better still, with a symbol of some kind, such as ▶ or ■ that will stand out from the text and enhance retention.

The second round (2) involves knowledge testing and the making of brief notes of the main things to remember.

The third round (3) will see a further reduction of these notes to lists that can be memorised. Try to memorise research references and examples to go with each topic, for example:

Change management might comprise these final notes (before going into the examination):

1 Change process: need for change – possible courses of action (*Organising for Success in the 21st Century*, CIPD research report). Communication – implementation – review.

2 Change models: (try to learn two in some detail) (Kurt) Lewin (*Field Theory in Social Science*, 1951, New York, Harper & Row); Beckhard (BECKHARD R. *Organisational Development Strategy and Models*, 1969, Addison-Wesley) and for *contrast* Beer (BEER M., EISENSTAT R. and SPECTOR B. 'Why change programs don't produce change', *Harvard Business Review*, Nov/Dec 1990, pp158–166).

3 Resistance – barriers and overcoming them ('Management, change and choice' , in BURNES B., *Managing Change*, 1992, London, FT Pitman Publishing).

4 Brief overview of at least two examples to show differing scenario. There are case studies in all the texts mentioned above. Particularly recent is the CIPD research report *Organising for Success in the 21st Century*, 2002, CIPD.

If this schedule is to be followed, revision would need to begin eight to ten weeks before the examination.

Once the schedule is decided, stick to it. Getting in front of schedule allows for slowing down or taking some time out. Falling behind means building in some extra time, but at least there is advance warning.

Where to do it

When and where to revise again depends on the individual, but it is important to concentrate, and the activity is better approached from the 'little and often' perspective. If fortunate enough to have study leave, students might like to think about taking a day a week for five weeks, rather than a whole week. Days and days spent at home trying to revise and learn may be wasted because the intensity is too great.

Find somewhere that is comfortable and, ideally where papers can be left at the end of each session. Be selfish in this, it is only for a fixed period of time after all. It is easier than most people think to make time during the day, by videoing favourite soaps and watching them later in the evening or at the weekend, and is it essential to watch the evening news at 6 pm *and* at 10 pm? If home is not a suitable venue, then try the workplace either before everyone else arrives, or after they have gone home. Local or college and university libraries can also provide a haven of peace and should not offer many distractions. Make use of car, train and bus journeys for reading or listening (remember the idea of audio tapes of the key points?). Remember to keep testing knowledge throughout – thinking about how answers will be expressed in the examination.

Finally, allow some rewards for these sterling efforts! A glass of wine, a packet of chocolate biscuits....

REFERENCES

[1]HANDY C. *Understanding Organisations*, 1985, London Penguin

[2]KANTER R.M. *The Change Masters*, 1984, N.S.W. Allen & Unwin

[3]STEWART R. *Managers and their Jobs*, 1967, Basingstoke Macmillan

[4]PUGH D. and HICKSON D. *Writers on Organisations*, 1996, London Penguin

[5]ARMSTRONG M. *Managing Activities*, 1999, London IPD, Foreword

[6]ibib.

• PRACTICE EXAMINATION QUESTIONS

Whatever the rights and wrongs, and whatever our point of view about them, if CIPD membership is sought through study, there will be some examinations. More candidates pass Managing Activities than fail! The average pass rate is around 60 per cent. The examiner does want candidates to pass, but your chances can be improved considerably by following a few simple guidelines.

Up to now this CIPD Revision Guide has focused mostly on gaining the knowledge needed to pass. We should now consider how that knowledge is presented. This includes not only the ability to recall and apply learning, but also how to 'handle' the examination process.

Details of the examination number and centre will be received in advance of 'the day'. Candidates must check the date, time and name of the paper and familiarise themselves with the route to the location, including traffic congestion blackspots, train strikes, and the venue itself, car parking, catering facilities and so on. Don't add to stress by being stuck in traffic or unable to find a parking space. Allow plenty of time, plan to arrive early.

Once in the examination room, check that the question paper is the right one and read the instructions carefully. As can be seen from past papers, there is an initial reading time of ten minutes, during which no writing is allowed. Remember there are two sections to the paper:

Section A is a choice of two from three possible questions.

Section B is a series of ten short questions from which seven are to be answered.

The invigilator will explain the start and finish times and will announce when reading the paper can begin and then again when to begin to write the answers. The reading time encourages candidates to look at all the questions, and if reading is not finished at the end of the ten minutes, carry on. Permission to write after ten minutes does not mean that it is compulsory. At this stage, anxiety is understandable so it is crucial to concentrate on what the question is asking in terms of knowledge, context and format.

You will find below in this CIPD Revision Guide a copy of the May 2003 Managing Activities examination paper, together with some guidelines about the expected and actual answers, but for now we shall continue to deal with some more general points. Read the instructions and the questions carefully. More often than not, candidates fail because they do not answer the question that has been set. What topic or topics are to be covered in the answer? What is the context and what form of answer is required? Marks have been allocated for all the dimensions of the answer, so it is essential to meet all requirements. The order in which questions are answered is up to the candidate, but it is not advisable to be thinking about these things for the first time when five minutes into the time allocated to demonstrate ability and brilliance!

Candidates have differing views on whether to answer Section A or Section B first, but whatever the sequence just remember to allocate equal time to each section as they carry equal marks. This is where getting to know how long it takes to write a page of A4 will pay dividends. The questions within sections also carry equal marks, so manage the time within Section A and Section B as well as across the whole paper. Always leave some space at the end of each answer. If there is any time to spare, it may be possible to add to or change the content, and this will enable the examiner to see more clearly what is being attempted in the answer.

A further dilemma for candidates is whether to answer on their 'best known' topics first; first of all, don't rush to answer where a topic is mentioned before considering the context and format required. A candidate may know all about risk assessment in theory, but their ability to implement it in the voluntary sector or across a multinational financial services organisation might let them down. Some candidates will attempt questions where knowledge is not so strong at the start, when they are less tired.

Whatever the order, the first essential is to draft an answer plan that includes the main points (perhaps as a series of headings, or in a mind map) and indicate the references and illustrations to be included. Although it may seem to be taking valuable time, it is worth considering drafting all answer plans first and then going back and writing the full answer. This is something that needs to be thought through in advance of the examination and to have been practised during revision. While Section B answers are by definition quite short anyway, drafting an answer plan for all ten may reveal that some are better to be tackled than appeared to be the case at first sight. It is also worth considering drafting all answer plans first and then going back to write the full answer, because when candidates are feeling more tired towards the end of the two hours the fact that there are already notes to refer to may help not only memory, but also confidence. The examiner may also take the answer plan into account, if time runs out.

■ Structuring the answer

It seems like an obvious truth, but the question must be answered in full. A pass is unlikely if only part of the question is answered or, as some candidates seem to prefer, the given answer is to the question they would like to have been asked!

Is the question asking for:

- Both sides of the argument, or just one?

- Recommendations to be included?

- Action plan to be drafted?

- A specific format, eg presentation, briefing notes?

The question is likely to indicate by whom this answer/advice is needed, eg CIPD students, chief executive officer, business associate. Please write in a way that is appropriate for this audience. Questions may also indicate a 'role' and must be answered as someone in that position would respond, eg HR director, employee reward consultant, CIPD student on placement.

It should be clearer now that the CIPD wants candidates (and prospective members) to be able to answer in a variety of roles and contexts that indicate potential as a thinking performer, not only at present, but for the future.

■ Incorporating references and examples

Many candidates seem to have difficulty with references, but whether this is because they have not done any background reading, or they are shy of quoting others is not always clear. The PDS standards require an awareness of current and emergent research, theory and writers in the area of study. Do not be 'ashamed' to cite someone else's ideas and experiences as long as they are correctly referenced. It will enhance the answer, show that there is a body of evidence to support the views and recommendations, and help individuals and organisations to see that there may be other ways of doing things. The phrasing of questions may require references to research, theory, and so on, but even if it is not explicit in the wording of the question, use such references wherever and whenever possible.

Examples are also encouraged to illustrate the points that are being made.

Examples are requested because they clearly demonstrate understanding (or not) of what is being written about. Take the following question from a past paper:

'Give three examples of methods that can be used to communicate the need for better safety practices in your workplace.'

Many candidates wrote about the need to motivate and incentivise employees who often pay little regard to safety, especially in an office environment, but this is only a situation or scenario. A good example came from a candidate who made this point and went on to describe a scheme that existed in their own organisation; this was a safety quiz on the intranet with a weekly £10 prize for the winner; 85 per cent of employees took part. Prior to this training on health and safety, which was offered in a half-hour training session, had attracted only around 20 percent of staff. The two covered the same ground, but the communication method and small reward were obviously preferred by employees.

Answering technique

Finally, examination performance will improve with practice of answering technique:

- practise writing answers against the clock, to give a better idea of how long it takes to write a page

- check practice answers by marking them (or getting someone else to mark them) against the criteria listed in the questions and earlier in this guide.

- take advantage of any mock examinations run by the study centre.

All of these will improve confidence and likelihood of success.

■ Answering the PDS Managing Activities Paper, May 2003

This was the first examination paper for PDS Managing Activities, though a specimen paper was previously produced and circulated to centres to give an indication of what it would look like. The main new feature was the change in the Section B requirements from answering eight questions from eight (PQS) to answering seven questions from ten (PDS).

This chapter gives an overview of the paper and what was expected of the candidate. It is unlikely that there will ever be a specific 'one and only' answer to any of the questions, but the examiner will always provide guidelines for reviewers, markers and moderators of question papers to indicate what he or she has in mind.

The actual examination paper is reproduced here question by question. It can be seen in full at the end of the chapter.

Section A

Section A comprises three questions, of which candidates must answer two.

Question 1

Prepare a one-day workshop for line managers that will improve their effectiveness in meetings. Outline and justify the content and methods you would use and explain how you would ensure that the managers put their learning into practice on return to the workplace.

Most managers agree that while meetings can be necessary, much time can be wasted at them. The meeting may not have been necessary at all, or it took too long and failed to make progress.

This question placed significant demands on the candidate if they chose to answer it fully and well. First of all, the candidate had to know about meetings and in particular, how to run effective ones. They were thus expected to include:

- send out the agenda in good time

- ensuring only those people who needed to be there were present

- good-quality minutes were taken

- an effective chair was appointed.

This latter point is probably the most crucial, and better candidates would be expected to place some extra emphasis on this.

The particular mix of people attending any meeting is also crucial and could be illustrated through allusion to Belbin's typology[1] or the work of Margerison and McCann[2].

In addition to knowledge of how to make meetings effective, the question puts several other demands on the candidate, in particular the design of such a workshop to suit the specific audience. Line managers are action people and generally respond well to plenty of activity and experiential learning. If they are going to spare a whole day, then they need to get something out of it. Pre-workshop activity will encourage them to focus on examples of good and bad practice and to examine their own strengths and weaknesses. They should also be encouraged to identify their reasons for attending and what they hope to achieve. It would be appropriate to ask them to complete a learning-style questionnaire to inform the choice of methods.

Much management development is self-development, as all managers have different learning capacities and work that puts various demands on them. So when it comes to the final section of the question, 'How would you ensure that the managers put their learning into practice in the workplace?', some control might be proposed by the trainer, but individual action plans would be the preferred approach. A follow-up session would keep the plan on track, as might an e-mail, phone call or postcard. If a group of managers work together or meet fairly regularly, then an electronic notice board or just an e-mail group address list might encourage a further exchange of experiences and suggestions. So much of management development is self-development that any proposals must be flexible in terms of time and accessibility. Putting learning into practice was an essential feature of this question as this is often where the benefits of such a workshop are depleted.

Question 2

You have been consulted by the Management Standards Centre to participate in their review of Management Standards. You are asked to provide them with your definition of management in the 21st century and a list of what you consider will be the main functions of management over the next two decades. A brief explanation of each point should be given, indicating the evidence that led to its inclusion.

New Management Standards are due to be published during 2003. The Centre for Management Standards has suggested the following definition: 'to provide direction, gain commitment, facilitate change and achieve results through the efficient creative and responsible use of resources'. The main competencies would include:

1 develop vision, gain commitment, provide governance

2 lead innovation, manage change

3 lead business operations and projects, meet customer needs

4 build relationships, develop networks and partnerships

5 manage self

6 manage financial resources, procure products and/or services, manage physical resources and technology, manage information and knowledge.

Candidates were expected to reflect this interpretation, as they are based on the current standards. Answers also needed to be forward-looking with up-to-date contemporary supporting evidence, and reference to some of the older, more established texts such as Peter Senge's *The Fifth Discipline*, Tom Peters's *Thriving on Chaos* or Charles Handy's *Age of Unreason*, whose ideas continue to have currency.

Question 3

In a call centre absence rates through illness have been increasing for operatives who are expected to meet demanding targets for answering calls and securing orders. You have been asked by the supervisor to investigate the causes.

- How would you conduct the investigation?

- What causes might you expect to identify?

- What action would you subsequently recommend and why?

Health and Safety and conditions of work were the focus here. The context of the question is the call centre, which has been likened to a modern production line, and its staff to battery hens. Within this setting the questions required an examination of monitoring absence and the reasons for illness, which it was indicated may be due to stress and/or poor work design. In terms of the investigation, candidates were expected to propose both qualitative and quantitative techniques. There should also have been some external benchmarking, certainly within the call centre environment. A useful source of data here would be the CIPD annual survey on absenteeism report or IDS publications.

The actual causes would not be known until the investigation is complete, but it is likely that they might include:

- Physical symptoms such as headaches, backache and RSI from poor workstation layout or job design

- Psychological stress from targets and deadlines that are unrealistic, and a lack of ownership and control over the work.

Actions were needed to address the causes, but whatever was recommended should be urgent, though there may be a mix of short- and longer-term solutions. In the short term, a risk assessment exercise and return-to-work interviews would be viable suggestions. In the longer term, regular monitoring of absence as part of Health and Safety procedures, regular risk assessment and the implementation and implications of Health and Safely legislation should be considered.

While short-term measures are reactive, the longer term should put an emphasis on the proactive.

Finally, whatever the recommendations, any costs must be weighed against lost business, poor customer service, increased levels of pay for sickness and cover, and possibly increasing labour turnover costs. In short – the business case.

Section B

Question 1

'How do you get your staff to listen to you?' asks a colleague. 'With mine everything I say seems to go in one ear and out the other.' What constructive advice will you give her?

Answers to this question should have included the fact that there could be several causes for the problem, and direct the colleague to ask herself some questions based on respected communication models or theories regarding communication breakdown, Torrington and Weightman,[3] for example. This is an approach that will help the colleague to deal not only with the current situation but also in the future. In addition, good answers might point out some of the most common barriers and offer suggestions on that basis, for example:

- when does she communicate? Timing is important. Praise and correction need to be immediate – a briefing for next week is not good at 5.45 pm on Friday.

- how does she communicate? E-mails are not always read or acted upon, even though they are a convenient way of sending information quickly to a large number of people.

Management style could be alluded to, but would attract marks only if it was in addition to the main focus on communication.

Question 2

Outline and justify the main points you would expect to be made in a presentation about the importance of meeting deadlines.

Meeting deadlines has important connotations for managers, ranging from avoiding stress to keeping customers. Getting things done on time can be the most stressful activity that managers engage in. Working with and through others makes getting it right even more important. The major point made in the answer must have been the importance of meeting the deadline, and reasons would include:

- ensures business objectives are met, thus helping company growth and profitability

- the achievement of targets may affect earnings in terms of profit-related or performance-related pay

- customer care and satisfaction can be gained or improved

- quality assurance, quality control and continuous improvement will suffer if deadlines slip

- individual and team motivation will improve as success is achieved.

In addition, candidates might go on to discuss how to ensure that deadlines are met, but this is subsidiary to the main answer.

The question referred to a presentation, but gave no specific duration or audience. Some reference should be made to this format, and it would be permissible for candidates to identify a target audience if it gives a better definition to their answer. The main requirement is both to outline and justify the points being made. Failure to do one or the other will always result in lost marks.

Question 3

You are preparing to give a talk to the local branch of the Institute of Directors entitled 'How Human Resource Management can make a contribution to competitive advantage'. Justify the sources of evidence you will utilise and outline what your main points will be.

HR's contribution to competitive advantage may not be a topic that the candidate automatically associates with managing activities. This question, however, demanded consideration of the strategic contribution and relates to the 'thinking performer' concept. It was very much about what directors and chief executives want to know and will be influenced by. The use of the HR dimension emphasises the importance of people, and is also something which those aspiring to become members of CIPD should be familiar with. This latter point is important as it allows candidates to concentrate on the audience and the sources of evidence.

For a talk to IOD members, the wise manager will want to respect their status (real or perceived!), and should indicate that he/she is aware that members may be directors of large or small, public or private organisations. They will all be looking for value for money/added value, managing change and competitive advantage through people or otherwise. This might have prompted the inclusion of topics such as knowledge management, recruiting for attitude, cost-effective contracts and so on. Candidates must be mindful that this is neither the Employee Resourcing nor Managing People examination paper. The nature of the talk should be slick and include factual evidence from successful companies. A good recent source of cases would be the *Sunday Times* '100 best companies to work for' or the CIPD's *People Make the Difference.*[4] There would also be respect for *Harvard Business Review* or *The Economist* or *Financial Times.*

Question 4

Identify three major team-working characteristics and explain why they are important for quality enhancement and improvement.

It is extremely important to realise that this question has two distinct, but vital, parts and candidates need to link their knowledge of teams with quality. Detailed descriptions of how teams work in a general context would not attract many marks, neither would reference to characteristics that are not specific or exclusive to teams. All candidates should know at least three, and these might include:

- mix of skills, experiences and insights

- flexibility of response, self-determination

- continuity of service and support

- speedy decision-making

- synergy.

Answers should explain how these qualities or characteristics impact on quality, ideally using examples of good practice. Quality circles or colleague circles would provide a good model – examples of the former can be found in most Japanese and many other manufacturing companies. Colleague circles would be found in service industries, particularly retail.

Question 5

Evaluate the evidence that mission statements positively affect organisational life.

A mission statement sets out, in broad terms, why an organisation exists. It should, therefore, be the driving force of all activity. It can impact on some if not all of the following areas:

- customer perception

- shareholder perception

- increased employee motivation owing to clarity of purpose and behavioural guidance

- improved management through setting of goals and achievement of targets.

This identifies the potential for a positive effect. A good illustration of the actual impact of the mission statement can be found in the Blood Transfusion Service, which highlights the process necessary for a positive outcome. This process includes:

- determination of the mission by representatives of all levels and areas

- communication and buy-in

- monitoring and evaluation of the impact.

The way in which the above process is enacted forms a major part of the evaluation. Mission statements must be 'short and memorable, show the business you are in and how you aim to meet customer needs'.

Question 6

You have received an e-mail from your new quality supervisor. She wants to know what is meant by 'zero defects' and whether realistically it can be achieved. She also wonders if you would be able to offer a comparable quality assurance model. Draft a comprehensive reply that explains zero defects and its application and outline an alternative model that one might want to consider.

Candidates needed to be confident in their knowledge to answer this question well – it offers no hiding places!

Zero defects is the term coined by and associated with Crosby to describe the key performance standard:

- quality means conformance not elegance

- there is no such thing as a quality problem

- no such thing as the economics of quality

- always easier to do the job right first time

- the only performance measure is the cost of quality

- the only performance standard is zero defects.

Realistically, candidates may have felt it more appropriate to the manufacturing sector, and 'right first time' has been shown to be achievable in many organisations throughout the world. The question does not specify a sector, so better candidates may have wished to comment on its effectiveness or achievability in their own or another organisation with which they are familiar. There are plenty of alternatives, ranging from statistical techniques to Total Quality Management, ISO 9001 and even IiP.

EFQM is a good all-purpose model, and even if the quality supervisor did not want to go for the Kitemark, the criteria could be adopted as in-house guidelines. The nine criteria offer a variety of measures such as customer comments, staff surveys, financial results and recovery rates.

Question 7

You are attempting to convince the senior management team of the importance of investing in a customer care programme. An important feature of this will be the links between customer care and financial performance. What would you include in the memo you are drafting that will convince them of the positive impact of such links?

Customer care and financial performance links can be difficult to quantify, but will be important in, for example, persuading managers and other staff of its importance and the need to ensure staff are fully trained to maximise the benefit.

Stone[5] lists:

- less lost business

- fewer lost customers

- repeat sales

- scope to increase revenue and profit by targeting sales to customer needs

- better, more efficient arrangements for service delivery and therefore lower staff and administration costs.

There needed to be consideration in the answer of how to make the case persuasive. Armstrong lists:[6]

- define objective

- get the facts

- marshal the argument

- anticipate objections

- find out what the senior management team wants

- look for the hidden agenda

- prepare a simple and attractive case

- make the audience party to your idea

- sell the benefits positively

- take immediate action.

There was a real need for candidates to read this question thoroughly, to ensure they picked up on the links between customer service and financial performance, not just on the importance of investing in a customer care programme.

The examples and evidence cited should be based on the premiss – 'following the introduction of a customer care programme company *x* saw its profits rise/its costs reduce by *y*'.

Candidates could also use as part of the argument the service/profit cycle developed by Reichheld.

Question 8

The Health and Safety policy statement for an organisation should be a declaration of the intention of the employer to safeguard the health and safety of employees. What major principles should it emphasise? Your Chief Executive Officer (CEO) asks you to analyse, with justifications, the reasons for this emphasis. Give your reply.

This question asked for information and supporting arguments. What are the major principles and why?

- the safety of the employees and the public is of paramount importance

- safety takes precedence over expediency

- the development and implementation of Health and Safety procedures should involve all staff

- Health and Safety legislation will be complied with in the spirit as well as the letter of the law

- all staff must be given Health and Safety training.

The reasons would encompass:

- all staff must realise their part

- all staff must have a responsibility for their own safety and that of others, and to understand and follow procedures

- commitment to Health and Safety brings financial benefits through quality performance and products.

Answers should be presented in a way that is appropriate for the Chief Executive Officer, who would be likely want to 'do the right thing' with minimum cost and disruption. A mention of the personal liability of the CEO in Health and Safety would have some impact, for example the issue of 'corporate manslaughter'.

Question 9

A business has grown rapidly in size and in the acquisition of new sites. What evidence is there to suggest that a decentralised organisational structure may now be more appropriate than the current centralised one?

The evidence should have been drawn from two main sources – textbook models and actual examples of decentralised businesses. The former may have included the relative characteristics of centralised and decentralised, but must also relate these to this specific context and not just list them or draw a diagram with no explanation. Points that would be relevant and well made could include:

- quicker decision-making
- faster response times
- closer to customer
- can reflect the nature of the locality and local community.

Examples from organisational practice might be generalised or specific, but needed to highlight what benefits were gained and, if possible, how these had been quantified. An example recently came from a national fitness centre/leisure activities company that decentralised its operations and found that quicker decisions, easier access to information, and better communications resulted. Staff motivation improved, absenteeism fell from 12 per cent to 4 per cent, and financial performance improved. It is permissible for candidates to discuss the downside of decentralisation but only *after* they have answered on the positive effects, not instead.

Question 10

How would you advise senior management to manage major change in your organisation in a positive way, ensuring that they pay due regard to the many models of change that abound and to the lessons learned by other organisations?

Candidates might have applied any theoretical approach or model, with appropriate referencing. They may also have described a well-executed example of change management to prove their point. The advice to senior managers must convince them that what is being proposed is tried and tested.

Examples of models abound: Lewin, Beckhard, Thurley, and Beer are all contenders. Rosbeth Moss Kanter's *The Change Masters* is also worth a mention.

The main principles will include:

- determine the reasons for change and the desired outcomes and objectives
- plan
- communicate to staff
- listen to feedback and review progress and direction.

■ The Managing Activities Paper, May 2003

Chartered Institute of Personnel and Development

Professional Development Scheme

Core Management

Managing Activities

May 2003

6 May 2003   09:50–12:00 hrs

Time allowed – Two hours and ten minutes (including ten minutes' reading time).

Answer two questions in Section A and seven of the ten questions in Section B. Please write clearly and legibly.

Questions may be answered in any order.

Equal marks are allocated to each section of the paper.
Within Section B equal marks are allocated to each question.

If a question includes reference to 'your organisation', this may be interpreted as covering any organisation with which you are familiar.

You are likely to fail the examination if:

*   **you fail to answer seven questions in Section B and/or**
*   **you achieve less than 40 per cent in any section.**

SECTION A

Answer ANY TWO questions in this section.

1 Prepare a one-day workshop for line managers that will improve their effectiveness in meetings. Outline and justify the content and methods you would use and explain how you would ensure that the managers put their learning into practice on return to the workplace.

2 You have been consulted by the Management Standards Centre to participate in their review of Management Standards. You are asked to provide them with your definition of management in the 21st century and a list of what you consider will be the main functions of management over the next two decades. A brief explanation of each point should be given, indicating the evidence that led to its inclusion.

3 In a call centre absence rates through illness have been increasing for operatives who are expected to meet demanding targets for answering calls and securing orders. You have been asked by the supervisor to investigate the causes.

   * How would you conduct the investigation?

   * What causes might you expect to identify?

   * What action would you subsequently recommend and why?

PLEASE TURN OVER

SECTION B

Answer SEVEN of the ten questions in this section. To communicate your answers more clearly you may use whatever methods you wish, for example diagrams, flowcharts, bullet points, so long as you provide an explanation of each.

1   'How do you get your staff to listen to you?' asks a colleague. 'With mine everything I say seems to go in one ear and out the other.' What constructive advice will you give her?

2   Outline and justify the main points you would expect to be made in a presentation about the importance of meeting deadlines.

3   You are preparing to give a talk to the local branch of the Institute of Directors entitled 'How Human Resource Management can make a contribution to competitive advantage'. Justify the sources of evidence you will utilise and outline what your main points will be.

4   Identify three major team-working characteristics and explain why they are important for quality enhancement and improvement.

5   Evaluate the evidence that mission statements positively affect organisational life.

6   You have received an e-mail from your new quality supervisor. She wants to know what is meant by 'zero defects' and whether realistically it can be achieved. She also wonders if you would be able to offer a comparable quality assurance model. Draft a comprehensive reply that explains zero defects and its application and outline an alternative model that she might want to consider.

7   You are attempting to convince the senior management team of the importance of investing in a customer care programme. An important feature of this will be the links between customer care and financial performance. What would you include in the memo you are drafting that will convince them of the positive impact of such links?

PLEASE TURN OVER

8   The Health and Safety policy statement for an organisation should be a declaration of the intention of the employer to safeguard the health and safety of the employees. What major principles should it emphasise? Your Chief Executive Officer (CEO) asks you to analyse, with justifications, the reasons for this emphasis. Give your reply.

9   A business has grown rapidly in size and in the acquisition of new sites. What evidence is there to suggest that a decentralised organisational structure may now be more appropriate than the current centralised one?

10 How would you advise senior management to manage major change in your organisation in a positive way, ensuring that they pay due regard to the many models of change that abound and to the lessons learned by other organisations?

END OF EXAMINATION

[1]BELBIN M. *Management Teams: Why they succeed or fail*, 1981, Oxford Heinemann

[2]MARGERISON C. and McCANN R. 'The Margenson-McCann team management resource theory and application', *International Journal of Manpower*, 1986, Vol. 7, No. 2

[3]TORRINGTON D. and WEIGHTMAN J. *Action Management*, 1991, IPM

[4]*People Make the Difference*, 1995, London IPD

[5]STONE M. 'Evaluating the profitability of customer service', in MARLEY P. (ed) *The Gower Handbook of Customer Service*, 1997, Vermont Gower

[6]ARMSTRONG M. *Managing Activities*,1999, London IPD

• FEEDBACK ON EXAMINATION QUESTIONS

This chapter analyses the major strengths and weaknesses of candidates' actual responses to the questions. It might be worth noting that if all the advice given in Chapters 1, 2 and 3 were taken, this chapter might be unnecessary. The comments in this chapter should also be read in conjunction with the remarks in Chapter 5. There are still many unnecessary and avoidable weaknesses. These are summarised here and at the end of the chapter:

Answer the question

Answer the question

ANSWER THE QUESTION

ANSWER THE QUESTION.

And include the three Es:

Explanation

Examples

Evidence.

Section A

Section A is comprised of three questions, any two of which should be attempted. They are fairly complex in the demands placed on Students and may require a more discursive and detailed response than those in Section B.

Question 1

Prepare a one-day workshop for line managers that will improve their effectiveness in meetings. Outline and justify the content and methods you would use and explain how you would ensure that the managers put their learning into practice on return to the workplace.

Students showed thorough knowledge of how to make meetings effective and chose good delivery methods. They also justified their choice of methods. The main weakness came in two areas: first was failure to respond to the part of the question about putting the learning into practice. This is a crucial part of the process. Another problem with this transfer of learning was that candidates wanted to be too much in control mode, to observe the managers at work, to set objectives for them rather than with them. It would be much more effective if the managers were to manage the process themselves.

There were also too many answers that were too generalised. It is acceptable, even advisable to set out the answer under the headings:

1 Content outline and justification

2 Methods outline and justification

3 Putting the learning into practice.

Question 2

You have been consulted by the management standards centre to participate in their review of Management Standards. You are asked to provide them with your definition of Management in the 21st Century and a list of what you consider will be the main functions of management over the next two decades. A brief explanation of each point should be given, indicating the evidence that led to its inclusion.

This was the least popular of the three Section A questions, but the best answered. Again, the tasks were clearly identified:

1   give a definition of management in the 21st century

2   list the main functions of management over the next two decades

3   give a brief explanation of the above, citing sources of evidence.

Candidates who did all three did well. The weakest parts were the failure to give a definition or sources of evidence. Better candidates gave their definition and blended 'classical' theories, definitions and models of management with changes foreseen in the future. These included more coaching and facilitating, more visionary leadership and more relationship-building.

Question 3

In a call centre, absence rates through illness have been increasing for operatives who are expected to meet demanding targets for answering calls and securing orders. You have been asked by the supervisor to investigate the causes.

- How would you conduct the investigation?

- What causes might you expect to identify?

- What action would you subsequently recommend and why?

Most candidates recognised this as a question about Health and Safety and addressed all three bullet points. Those who responded purely from the perspective of objective-setting did not pass.

Failure to include both qualitative and quantitative research into the problem also resulted in poor marks. Better candidates looked not only inside their own organisation but externally to other call centres or sources of data on general absence rates. The causes were wide ranging and by and large relevant. Actions grew from the causes and were again pragmatic and logical, with candidates considering short- and long-term implications.

Section B

This section gave many candidates the most problems as they failed time and time again to answer the question concisely and thus threw away marks.

Question 1

'How do you get your staff to listen to you?' asks a colleague. 'With mine, everything I say seems to go in one ear and out the other.' What constructive advice will you give her?

Candidates offered sensible suggestions in the main, but failed to suggest that some diagnosis of the causes might be needed to ensure improvement. Those who cited models of communication gave the most comprehensive answers.

Question 2

Outline and justify the main points you would expect to be made in a presentation about the importance of meeting deadlines.

Many candidates failed to get a good mark for question 2 because they did not answer it. The context of the presentation scenario was ignored.

Major problems came because candidates failed to write about the importance of meeting deadlines and wrote instead very full answers on what deadlines were and how to set them. Answers were very generalised and lacked the feel of the sharp, succinct response demanded in Section B.

Question 3

You are preparing to give a talk to the local branch of the Institute of Directors entitled 'How Human Resource Management can make a contribution to competitive advantage'. Justify the sources of evidence you will utilise and outline what your main points will be.

This question was quite popular, but very poorly answered. Candidates failed to take the audience into account and completely ignored the request for sources of evidence. It is not possible to detect whether this is because candidates lack knowledge, or misread the question. The candidates themselves will know. Candidates must become more proficient at making a case to a non-HR audience.

Question 4

Identify three major team-working characteristics and explain why they are important for quality enhancement and improvement.

There were two major faults here:

- failure to give three characteristics

- failure to link with, or in some cases, even mention quality enhancement and improvement.

This meant that few marks could be allocated. It is a great pity that students reduce their chances of success by ignoring what the question asks, or by answering an alternative question that they have set for themselves. Candidates frequently, but erroneously, chose three Belbin types, eg plant, chairman, shaper, monitor-evaluator as their three characteristics. Having a mix of types is important, but this mix is only one characteristic.

Question 5

Evaluate the evidence that mission statements positively affect organisational life.

Most candidates who attempted this question could define the mission statement. To pass they needed to go beyond that, however, and the better answers were really very good, giving informative examples of positive (and sometimes negative) impact in their own and other organisations. They were particularly critical of mission statements devised by senior executives (thus no 'buy-in' from staff) of which employees were largely ignorant.

Question 6

You have received an e-mail from your new quality supervisor. She wants to know what is meant by 'zero defects' and whether realistically it can be achieved. She also wonders if you would be able to offer a comparable quality assurance model. Draft a comprehensive reply that explains zero defects and its application and outline an alternative model that she might want to consider.

Many candidates attempted this question, though they clearly knew little, if anything, about zero defects and made no reference to whether or not it could be achieved. Alternative models were mentioned, but in very general terms. The supervisor would not have been much the wiser for reading them. So lack of knowledge contributed to failure here.

Question 7

You are attempting to convince the senior management team of the importance of investing in a customer care programme. An important feature of this will be the links between customer care and financial performance. What would you include in the memo you draft that will convince them of the positive impact of such links?

Candidates were well informed and knowledgeable about customer care. The main weaknesses in their answers were either:

- writing only about the importance of investing in a programme of customer care and failing to emphasise the links between customer care and financial performance, or

- being unable to cite any hard evidence showing the link between the two that might convince senior colleagues

Candidates seem to need more practice at expressing their knowledge in a given context.

Question 8

The Health and Safety policy statement for an organisation should be a declaration of the intention of the employer to safeguard the health and safety of employees. What major principles should it emphasise? Your Chief Executive Officer (CEO) asks you to analyse, with justifications, the reasons for this emphasis. Give your reply.

Many candidates answered this well, not only giving the principles, but analysing and justifying the emphasis too. Those candidates who did not do so well often confused principles with practices, indicating a lack of understanding of the terms and possibly a lack of strategic thinking when it comes to Health and Safety.

Question 9

A business has grown rapidly in size and in the acquisition of new sites. What evidence is there to suggest that a decentralised organisational structure may now be more appropriate than the current one?

Most candidates were able to distinguish between centralised and decentralised structures, and better ones applied that knowledge in the given context. Better answers sometimes went so far as to suggest that a 'mixed model' was more practical, with some areas still retained by head office. Good examples, from a wide range of sources, were given. Where students failed, it was invariably because they simply outlined what is meant by centralised and decentralised, and no more.

Question 10

How would you advise senior management to manage change in your organisation in a positive way, ensuring that they pay due regard to the many models of change that abound and to the lessons learned by other organisations?

This was a popular question, and many gave good answers that covered all parts of the question.

Candidates needed to:

- identify models and examples of good practice

- demonstrate knowledge of the managerial requirements of successful change management

- link those two aspects

- present the information in a way that would be acceptable to senior managers.

Those candidates who ignored or failed to include any of these points were likely to fail.

■ Summary

Answer the question

Be familiar with the professional standards and the examination set-up

Answer the question

Know at least 50 per cent of the Indicative Content well, and the other 50 per cent fairly well

Answer the question

Test yourself

Answer the question

Explain yourself

Answer the question

Support your arguments with evidence

Answer the question

Illustrate your answer with examples

Answer the question

Respond in the requested format

ANSWER THE QUESTION.

INDEX

- **NOTES**